PRE-WAR 1619–1819
Seeds of War Sown Early!

Africa. [...] hold of a ship [...] [...]ses of a strange and fearful land, at the hands of a white-skinned and cruel people. They say I am their slave, that they can buy and sell me at will. Surely no good can come from such an idea.—**Ella**, August 1619, Jamestown, VA

I is the Infant, from the arms
Of its fond mother torn,
And at a public auction sold
With horses, cows, and corn.

Z is a Zealous man, sincere,
Faithful, and just, and true;
An earnest pleader for the slave—
Will you not be so too?

We declare slavery illegal. —Rhode Island, 1652

Slaves are hereby declared "real estate." —State of Virginia, 1705

I have frequently seen [slaves] whipt to that degree that large pieces of their skin have been hanging down their backs, yet I never observed one of them to shed a tear.—**John Brickell**

I haven't anything to say against slavery. My old folks put my clothes on me…they gave me shoes and stockings and put them on me when I was a little boy. I loved them, and I can't go against them in anything. There were things I did not like about slavery on some plantations, whuppin' and sellin' parents and children from each other, but I haven't much to say. I was treated good.—**Samuel Riddick**

For months and months at a time we weren't allowed off the farm. Sometimes we would get as far as the gate and peep over. We were told that if we got outside the Padirollers would get us.—**Uriah Bennett**, slave

Slaves bring the judgment of Heaven on a country.—**George Mason**

I's just follow the finger. The white man point his finger and I follow it and do.—**Cuffee**, slave

In 1776 Thomas Jefferson signed the Declaration of Independence, which states "all men are created equal." Jefferson was a slave owner.

Declaration of Independence

SOLD!

I didn't come to America to get along with other people from all over and from other states. What do I care about them? I came for opportunity for me and my family. I'm all for fast progress, and bigger cities, and more work. What do I have in common with those hick farmers in the South—nothing. To the Devil with them!—**blacksmith**, Rhode Island

I was an early victim of slave trading. I was born in Benin, in what is now Nigeria, in 1745. At age 11, I was kidnapped from my family and sold into slavery. Later I was sold again to traders and chained on a slave ship bound for America. I was sold to a Virginia planter, and then to a British naval officer, and finally to a Philadelphia merchant who gave me the chance to buy my freedom. As a ship's steward, I traveled widely. I also worked to bring an end to the slave trade. In 1791, I wrote my autobiography.—**Gustavus Vassa**

Laws, I gots to be up at dawn's crack with the baby to head to the fields. That sun sho is hot. Massa says we gots to pick fast today. Cotton is back-breakin' work. It's just one row after another. Gots to stop to nurse the baby as I can, but so the 'seer can't see me.—**Lizzie**, 17, plantation slave

Eli Whitney invents the cotton gin, 1793.

Eli Whitney's invention of the cotton gin made it possible for farmers to make more money and harvest more cotton each year. But it also meant farmers needed more workers. So, they bought slaves from Africa to tend their fields. The cotton gin revolutionized farming…and slavery.

1619…1st slaves to America land in Virginia…1652…Rhode Island declares slavery illegal…1688…1st public protest of slave trade in Pennsylvania…1700

1829…A free black, David Walker, publishes an essay which encourages slaves to revolt. As a result, most southern states make it illegal to teach slaves to read and write…1830…Anti-Slavery Movement begins…1831…Maria Stewart is the first

The Fugitive Slave Act of 1793 demands the return of runaway slaves.

1820–1860 Antebellum="Before the War"

abolitionist: person who worked to do away with slavery

Slavery is a covenant with death and an agreement with hell.—abolitionist **William Lloyd Garrison**, *The Liberator*, Boston

I don't know why some people can't understand the unity of the South. We have our own identity and traditions. Cotton is my crop and I need my slaves to make a successful living. If those darn Yankees came down here they'd see it's a lot of hot, hard hand-labor, no machine to magically get our crop in and meet the worldwide demand for cotton. Cotton is King, after all!—**plantation owner**, South Carolina

Antislavery newspapers began in 1821 with white editor Benjamin Lundy's *Genius of Universal Emancipation*. It had six subscribers.

COTTON IS KING!

Some people say "The South was built on the backs of blacks."

It's like this: they's good massas and bad massas. Most white folks not slaves, but be about as po' as we slaves are! My plantation family's good to me.—**slave cook**, Louisiana

Slavery was sometimes called a "necessary evil" or the "peculiar institution."

Reveille is a bugle call that was used to wake up sleeping soldiers at sunrise. During the Civil War, the call was sounded between 4:45-6:00 in the morning! When the last note played, the flag was raised, a gunshot was fired, and the soldiers had to be dressed and ready for roll call.

A plot that involved 9,000 blacks, led by free black Denmark Vesey, was exposed in Charleston, South Carolina in 1822. Vesey and 36 others were executed.

I can't believe a man like that can be President of these United States! Andrew Jackson is nothing but a common man. Newspapers call him a "barbarian," "half-wit," and "tyrant," and I must say, I agree with them. The people got what they wanted, I guess...a low-class man running this whole nation!—**U.S. citizen**, 1828

Only one of every 20 Northerners was an active abolitionist.

I didn't have to be told that if a slave struck his master it meant death. Freeborn in North Carolina, but the son of a slave father, I knew slavery firsthand. My hatred of slavery drove me to Boston, where I sold old clothes and subscriptions to the *Freedom's Journal*. I burned to deliver my own message and in 1829 published my pamphlet, *Walker's Appeal.*—**David Walker**

For Sale

In 1831, slave Nat Turner led 70 blacks in a revolt that slaughtered 57 men, women, and children in rural Southampton County, Virginia. Troops rushed in to put down the uprising and killed over one hundred blacks—the innocent as well as the insurrectionists—in a savage massacre. Wild rumors and alarms swept through the South—could this happen again?!—**newspaperman**, North Carolina

I didn't know I was a slave until I found out I couldn't do the things I wanted.—Edmund, Georgia

I bet that was a shock!

...Virginia declares slaves are "property"...New York puts runaway slaves to death...1725 ...Virginia grants slaves right to form own church...1739...Slave black woman to lecture against slavery...William Lloyd Garrison publishes the first edition of the newspaper, Liberator, which called for emancipation of slaves...Nat Turner leads a slave rebellion in Southampton, Virginia...1833...The American and

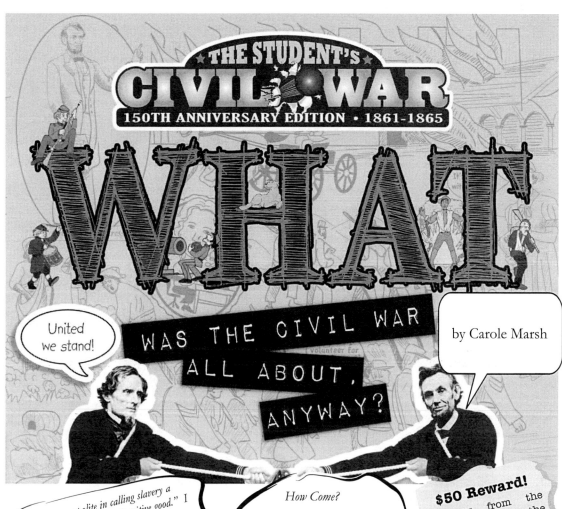

WHAT

WAS THE CIVIL WAR ALL ABOUT, ANYWAY?

by Carole Marsh

United we stand!

Southerners were polite in calling slavery a "necessary evil." I call slavery a "positive good." I stand by what I said in Congress—slavery is good for blacks!—**John C. Calhoun**, South Carolina senator, 1837

Boo! Boo!

I was born a slave. I worked long and hard for my master 22 years. I finally ran away, and been hiding in a small space in my grandmother's attic for seven years. I'm trying to get to the North and gain my freedom. I finally have my chance. A boat is going to take me there tonight. Perhaps by morning, I'll be free!— **Harriet Jacobs**, North Carolina

How Come?

When I was born I was black.
When I grew up I was black.
When I'm sick I'm black.
When I go out into the sun I'm black.
When I die I'll be black.

But you:
When you were born you were pink.
When you grow up you are white.
When you get sick you are green.
When you go out in the sun you are red.
When you go out in the cold you are blue.
When you die you turn purple.
And you call me colored?

sesquicentennial: (noun) [ses-kwi-sen-ten-ee-uhl] a 150th anniversary or its celebration

$50 Reward!

Ranaway from the Subscriber, living in the county of Edgecombe, NC, about eight miles north of Tarborough, on the 24th of August last, a negro fellow named Washington, about 24 years of age, 5 feet and 8 or 10 inches high, dark complexion, stout built, and an excellent field hand, no particular marks about him recollected.

Maybe he's on the railroad?

I was born on a plantation near Fayetteville, North Carolina, and I belonged to J.B. Smith. He owned about 30 slaves. When a slave was no good, he was put on the auction block in Fayetteville and sold.
—**Sarah Louise Augustus**

Runaways Held in the New Bern, NC, Jail

Two New Negro Men, the one named Joe, about 45 years of age...much wrinkled in the face, and speaks bad English. The other is a young fellow...speaks better English than Joe, whom he says is his father, has a large scar on the fleshy part of his left arm.... They have nothing with them but an old Negro cloth jacket and an old blue sailor's jacket without sleeves. Also...a Negro named Jack, about 23 years of age...of a thin visage, bleareyed...has six rings of his country marks around his neck, his ears are full of holes.

What man can make, man can unmake.— **Frederick Douglass**, abolitionist

rebellion in South Carolina; 44 slaves killed...1777...Vermont outlaws slavery...1783...Massachusetts outlaws slavery...1792...Kentucky joins Union as slave

the Female Anti-Slavery Societies are formed in Philadelphia...1833...Oberlin College is the first coed college founded to educate African Americans...1837...The first Anti-Slavery Convention of American Women is held in New

Copyright Year of Our Lord 2010
Carole Marsh/Gallopade International/Peachtree City, GA

I thought it was the Year of the Tiger.

No, that was last year. *Oh.*

Permission is hereby granted to the individual purchaser or classroom teacher to reproduce materials in this book for individual or classroom use only. Reproduction of these materials for an entire school or school system is strictly prohibited.

No part of this publication may be reproduced, stored in or introduced into a retrieval system, or transmitted, in any form or by any means (electronic, mechanical, photocopying, recording, or otherwise) without the prior written permission of the publisher of this book.

It takes an army to do a book. Here's ours:

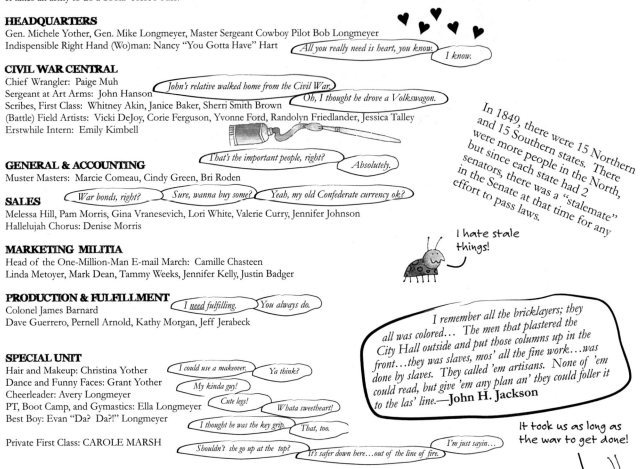

HEADQUARTERS
Gen. Michele Yother, Gen. Mike Longmeyer, Master Sergeant Cowboy Pilot Bob Longmeyer
Indispensible Right Hand (Wo)man: Nancy "You Gotta Have" Hart

All you really need is heart, you know. *I know.*

CIVIL WAR CENTRAL
Chief Wrangler: Paige Muh
Sergeant at Art Arms: John Hanson
Scribes, First Class: Whitney Akin, Janice Baker, Sherri Smith Brown
(Battle) Field Artists: Vicki DeJoy, Corie Ferguson, Yvonne Ford, Randolyn Friedlander, Jessica Talley
Erstwhile Intern: Emily Kimbell

John's relative walked home from the Civil War.

Oh, I thought he drove a Volkswagon.

That's the important people, right? *Absolutely.*

GENERAL & ACCOUNTING
Muster Masters: Marcie Comeau, Cindy Green, Bri Roden

SALES
War bonds, right? *Sure, wanna buy some?* *Yeah, my old Confederate currency ok?*

Melessa Hill, Pam Morris, Gina Vranesevich, Lori White, Valerie Curry, Jennifer Johnson
Hallelujah Chorus: Denise Morris

MARKETING MILITIA
Head of the One-Million-Man E-mail March: Camille Chasteen
Linda Metoyer, Mark Dean, Tammy Weeks, Jennifer Kelly, Justin Badger

PRODUCTION & FULFILLMENT
Colonel James Barnard

I need fulfilling. *You always do.*

Dave Guerrero, Pernell Arnold, Kathy Morgan, Jeff Jerabeck

SPECIAL UNIT
Hair and Makeup: Christina Yother
Dance and Funny Faces: Grant Yother
Cheerleader: Avery Longmeyer
PT, Boot Camp, and Gymnastics: Ella Longmeyer
Best Boy: Evan "Da? Da?!" Longmeyer

Private First Class: CAROLE MARSH

I could use a makeover. *Ya think?*

My kinda guy!

Cute legs! *Whata sweetheart!*

I thought he was the key grip. *That, too.*

Shouldn't she go up at the top? *I'm just sayin...*

It's safer down here...out of the line of fire.

In 1849, there were 15 Northern and 15 Southern states. There were more people in the North, but since each state had 2 senators, there was a "stalemate" in the Senate at that time for any effort to pass laws.

I hate stale things!

I remember all the bricklayers; they all was colored... The men that plastered the City Hall outside and put those columns up in the front...they was slaves, mos' all the fine work...was done by slaves. They called 'em artisans. None of 'em could read, but give 'em any plan an' they could foller it to the las' line.—**John H. Jackson**

It took us as long as the war to get done!

Carole Marsh Civil War and Other Sassy Books for Young Readers are available from your favorite school supply or teacher store, almost all of America's fine museum and park stores, at lovely bookstores everywhere, or if all else fails, direct from www.gallopade.com, or call 1-800-536-2GET (that's 2438), extension 11, Miss Cindy.

We have referred to a few of our favorite Internet and social media sites throughout this book. All trademarks are registered, and belong to their respective owners—none of whom sponsored nor endorsed this book, nor are affiliated with Gallopade International/Carole Marsh Books.

For further information, trade terms, rights sales, good recipes, advice, and more, please contact:
GALLOPADE INTERNATIONAL
6000 Shakerag Hill
Suite 314
Peachtree City, Georgia
30269

You mean like when the wife stood on the hill and waved her hankie welcoming her Johnny home from the war? *The very same!*

That's in the South, right? *They made up that town name, right?*

Yes. *Probably.*

See our bibliography
and more at
www.studentscivilwar.com

I had to try to put an end to this political battle! When the territory of California applied to join the Union in 1849—as a free state—the U.S. had half free and half slave states. To stop this madness, I introduced a bill that would let California be a free state. However, my Compromise of 1850 also said that any new state could choose to be free or slave based on "popular sovereignty" or what the people wanted. After all, a state should have the right to decide what it wants to be, right? My bill passed, but alas, it was only a temporary solution.—Senator **Henry Clay**, Kentucky

state...1793...The Fugitive Slave Act forces return of runaway slaves...Eli Whitney invents the cotton gin...1796...Tennessee joins Union as slave state...1800

York...1839...Joseph Cinque leads a successful revolt on the slave ship, Amistad...1850...Congress passes the Fugitive Slave Act requiring captured runaway slaves to be returned to their owners. Whites now hunt slaves for profit...

A Word from the Author

There's a song that goes *"War! What's it all about? Absolutely nothing!"*

However war is usually about *something*. As you know, the Revolutionary War was all about America wrenching herself away from the final grasp of her mother country of England. It was a war to secure freedom, a new nation, and a new way of life. Later, no one looked back and said, "Hey, maybe we shouldn't have fought that war."

Close to a hundred years after America's founding, people were restless. America was now about a lot of ways of life, many quite different from the others. You might be a plantation owner using slave labor to grow your cotton crop. You might be a mountain woman still living in the wilds of Appalachia. You could be a president trying to run the still new, young, ambitious, and sometimes, even cantankerous and disagreeable country.

Two of the major disagreements of the mid-1800s were slavery and states' rights versus federal rights. Some folks said that they could not survive without slave labor, that they were good to their slaves, and that slavery was now a necessary and permanent part of American life. Others said slavery was wrong and that there was no reason any human being should be owned by another. After all, wasn't America about freedom for all people?

Some Americans thought that states should be able to make their own decisions without so much interference from the federal government in Washington. (Sound familiar?) Other Americans insisted that's what Washington and the federal government were for: to keep all states fair and equal and to solve disputes.

You could say that lanky, teenage America had major growing pains! But America was no longer a "kid." America was at a serious crossroads. Would Americans fight their fellow Americans over these issues? Could such disagreements be resolved by talking, cooperation, compromise, and change? Or would we go to war?

What a curious turn of events—to believe you had to fight your fellow countrymen to the death! Wasn't there any other way? As we know today, getting along and solving problems is much better than going to war. Sometimes, if you are under attack, you may feel you have no choice but to go to war to defend your nation, or to defend others.

Let's just say it was complicated. By the spring of 1861, Americans were actually talking about going to war. They made it sound necessary, even exciting. Many believed it would be a quick war—with their side winning, naturally!

Of course, it didn't happen that way. It was a long war—four years—with terrible tragedies. Slavery was ended. But not before most people "took sides" and fought face-to-face, often against people they knew or were related to, until no one any longer felt that war was a good thing, not even a so-called "necessary" war.

We're right!   NO!, we're right!

...Free blacks petition Congress to end slavery...Armed slaves rebel in Virginia; most are executed...1803...Ohio joins Union as free state...U.S. buys Louisiana

1853...Sarah Parker Remond is refused a seat in the Howard Athenaeum in New York. She takes the case to the police court, and the defendants are fined...1854...Frances Ellen Watkins Harper delivers her first anti-slavery lecture and publishes

What eventually led to war was a long, drawn out, complex, contradictory set of circumstances, actions, misunderstandings, and oversights. Could we have ended slavery and preserved the union—without war? Think about this, for it may be your job to assess, decide, act or not act, or argue for or against some similar situation one day!

As you read, imagine being that person at that time, in that place during that event. How would you feel, what would you do, how would you change? Today, could we possibly still "stumble" into such a long war? Would around-the-clock news make a difference? Would gathering those who disagree around a table and negotiating work? Diplomacy? The Civil War contains a world of wondering!

What was the American Civil War about? What did it mean? Was there another way? Was it fun, exciting? Was it fair? Who won? Who lost? What would you have done? What do you think?

Why does it matter what *you* think? Because in the absence of diplomacy, cooperation, collaboration, compromise, understanding, honor, and integrity, it is war, not peace, that always looms on our horizon. The past was in their hands. The future is in yours.

Carole Marsh

Shakerag Hill
Peachtree City, Georgia

Reader,

After you read this book, you can go online to www.studentscivilwar.com and learn more.

Ask your school or public librarian to help you find resources for your age!

Did you hear? There are soldiers coming to town!

I've heard rumors of war going around lately. People whispering about soldiers, weapons, strategies. Some even say I've sparked their interest. They want to fight the South and end all the slavery right now. It's the book, I guess. When I wrote Uncle Tom's Cabin, I didn't expect it to be so controversial. I just knew the story needed to be told. I wanted people to know what life was really like for slaves, with good owners and bad owners from Southern and Northern towns. I think I really got people thinking. Most have never heard slavery described like this before.—**Harriet Beecher Stowe**

I am **Tom**, a fictional character from Ms. Stowe's famous book about how slaves were mistreated. In her story, I was murdered in cold blood by plantation overseer Simon Legree. Did such things happen in real life? Were they common or rare? What do you think?

*Nine months I was trying to get away.—***Solomon Northup**, *slave, born free in New York, kidnapped in 1841 and enslaved on a cotton plantation near Red River in Louisiana.*

I'm **Franklin Pierce**, elected president in 1852, but not strong enough to lead our nation through the gathering storm of war!

I find it so hard to believe that Americans might fight Americans! North or South, we are all countrymen, neighbors, brothers, sisters, friends—how can war be? And yet I feel this volcanic groundswell growing beneath the very soil of the land. Will all these eternal arguments over slavery, state versus federal rights, and more just grow louder until we are not talking, but fighting?—**new mother**, Georgia

This footer is a Civil War timeline on top and an African American timeline on the bottom.

Territory, fueling debate over slave status...1808...Congress outlaws slave trade; slavery persists...1812...Louisiana joins Union as slave state...1816... Indiana

her first book of verse ...1857...With the Dred Scott Decision, the U.S. Supreme Court denies citizenship to black people...1859...White abolitionist, John Brown, leads a raid at Harper's Ferry. He is captured and sentenced to death...1861...Civil

Table of
CONTENTS

Check out our extra 4 pages right after page 18!

I can't wait to read this book!

joins Union as free state...1817...Mississippi joins Union as slave state...1818...Illinois joins Union as free state...1819...Alabama joins Union as slave state...

War begins...Charlotte Forten Grimke becomes a volunteer teacher of freed men on St. Helena Island in South Carolina...1863...Harriet Tubman leads a military raid on the Combahee River in South Carolina and helps hundreds of slaves escape

WHAT

Was America's Civil War Really All About?

> Good question!
> What is war all about?
> An old song says, "Absolutely nothing!"

Many historians say that from 1861-1865, Americans fought a war on their own soil, fighting citizen against citizen (and often, brother against brother) because of:

- Slavery
- States' rights

> That's true, but let's add to this list. The "Civil" War was fought because:

In 1861, America was less than 100 years old, and we were still learning how to get along with each other.

Southerners had imported slaves starting in 1619, and felt that their plantation way of life had helped America grow, and that they could not survive without the help of slave labor.

The U.S. Constitution and all the great things our forefathers said were still new and open to interpretation. Americans had just gotten out from under overpowering British rule and many wanted their state to have the final say in things, not the federal government.

A lot of Americans were still, uh, pretty rough around the edges. Woodsmen. Frontiersmen. They were always ready for a good fight!

We were pretty opinionated and thought (whichever side we were on) OUR WAY was the right way. Most folks weren't much in the mood for diplomacy or compromise.

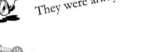

Northerners thought slavery was wrong and should be abolished. So did some Southerners!

 Wanna talk?

Nah, let's fight!

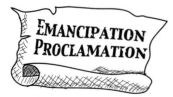

EMANCIPATION PROCLAMATION

> And you know, today, Americans are still growing and learning...and arguing, and that is healthy and good. Fighting to the death, uh, not so much.

8

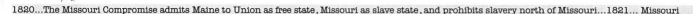

1820...The Missouri Compromise admits Maine to Union as free state, Missouri as slave state, and prohibits slavery north of Missouri...1821... Missouri

to freedom...1865...The Thirteenth Amendment abolishes slavery...The Freedmen's Bureau is established by Congress...1872...The Freedmen's Bureau is abolished by Congress...1877...The Hayes Compromise ends Reconstruction by

Them's FIGHTIN' WORDS!

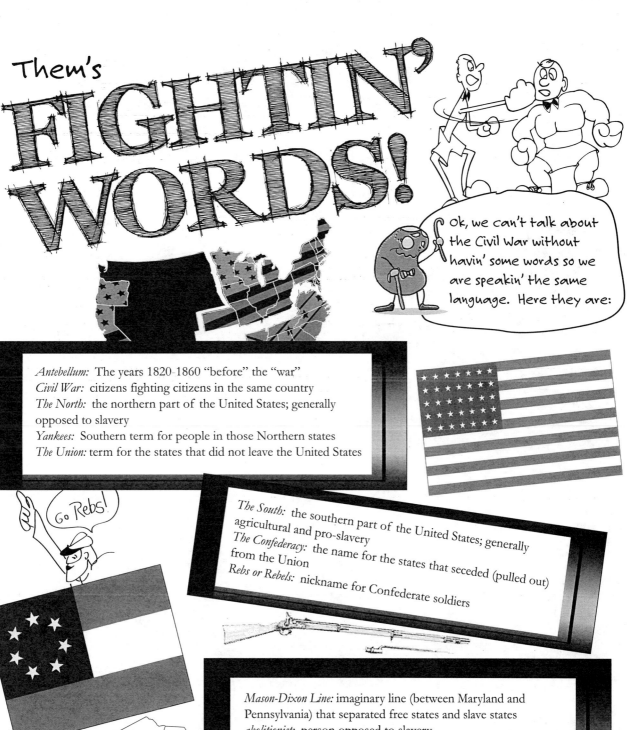

Ok, we can't talk about the Civil War without havin' some words so we are speakin' the same language. Here they are:

Antebellum: The years 1820–1860 "before" the "war"
Civil War: citizens fighting citizens in the same country
The North: the northern part of the United States; generally opposed to slavery
Yankees: Southern term for people in those Northern states
The Union: term for the states that did not leave the United States

Go Rebs!

The South: the southern part of the United States; generally agricultural and pro-slavery
The Confederacy: the name for the states that seceded (pulled out) from the Union
Rebs or Rebels: nickname for Confederate soldiers

Mason-Dixon Line: imaginary line (between Maryland and Pennsylvania) that separated free states and slave states
abolitionist: person opposed to slavery
emancipation: the freeing of slaves
secession: to leave the Union of "United States" in order to form a new government; this was illegal
Reconstruction: the years after the Civil War when the states reunited, rebuilt, and recovered

It was hard work!   VERY!

PA
MD   DE
The Mason-Dixon Line

Compromise blocks extension of slavery above latitudinal line of 36°30' north...1822...Slaves revolt in South Carolina; 37are hanged...1827...New York

withdrawing federal troops from the South...1880...Post Reconstruction era begins...The policy of white supremacy in the South leaves black people segregated, disenfranchised (without opportunity), and oppressed...1895...First National

IMAGINE IT...

America is a land of opportunity! I came here to do what I want to do, how I want to do it!

Opportunity? Not for me! I'm not free, never will be!

Our Northern cities are what keep America up and running—we're important! **—Businessman**

Our Southern plantations feed America—you'd starve without our crops! We need more slaves, not no slaves. **— Plantation Owner**

I live in the South. I don't own any slaves.

FREE THEM

Cotton is King!

Free the slaves!

The truth was there were all "flavors" of Americans with all "flavors" of opinions. Some Southerners opposed slavery. Some Northerners did not like the already "freed" slaves in their states. Other Northerners just wanted slavery to stay in the South, and not come to their states. Even some slaves feared how they would survive if free, although most were eager to be free.

outlaws slavery…1828…South Carolina insists states can void federal laws…1830…Congress debates states' rights vs. federal government…1831…Abolitionist

Seeds of DISTRUST

And so, the plot thickened! Many people plodded along with their hard-working lives, with no reason or time to do anything but survive. Others joined together to proclaim that they had the best idea or only way for Americans to behave. Some folks discussed issues calmly. Others yelled and screamed loudly, often on paper.

Antislavery abolitionists sometimes called slaveholders names.

When they came South to do this, they were often tarred and feathered!

Uh, look out below!

William Lloyd Garrison

The Liberator
Slavery is a covenant with death and an agreement with hell.
- Editor

Barbarians!

You're un-American!

Sinners!

I was hoping he was dishing out free dirt.

I'm a Free-Soiler. No, I don't give away dirt—I believe that any state, old or new, that wants to have slavery should be able to choose to do so.

Abolitionists actually were a very small part of the North, but they made a lot of noise and so people listened.

No! No! No! No! No!

Does anyone care what we think?

Sounds like dirty pool to me!

William Lloyd Garrison publishes The Liberator…Slave rebellion in Virginia leads to tougher slave laws…1832…Congress passes new tariff law, benefiting

College of Pennsylvania…1909…The NAACP is founded…1920…The Nineteenth Amendment gives women the right to vote…1935…Federal Writers' Project established by Franklin Roosevelt…fieldworkers were assigned to travel through

Armed Camps and Underground RAILROADS

And so, as the years and the arguing went on, Southerners who had slaves defended their need for this labor. Northern abolitionists and others insisted that slavery put all Americans' freedoms at risk.

Let's be wise and compromise.

No! No! No! No! No!

Can't you see democracy is the only way to be?

No! No! No! No! No!

You're guilty of treason, Mr. Meason!

You lie, Mr. Bly!

Can we talk?

No! No! No! No! No!

As both sides stuck to their stubborn guns, emotions heated up. In the meantime, many slaves trudged along the Underground Railroad, not willing to wait to be "freed."

Some slaves escaped on the secret route known as the Underground Railroad.

FREEDOM

I guess it's too late for tall fences to make good neighbors, huh?

Northern industry…South Carolina nullifies federal edict, calls for secession…President Jackson declares no states may leave Union…1833…Lucretia Mott

Southern states to gather life histories of ex-slaves…1940…Ella Jo Baker, a dedicated organizer in the freedom movement, begins work in the South as field secretary of the NAACP…1941…Civil Rights Movement begins…Thousands of black

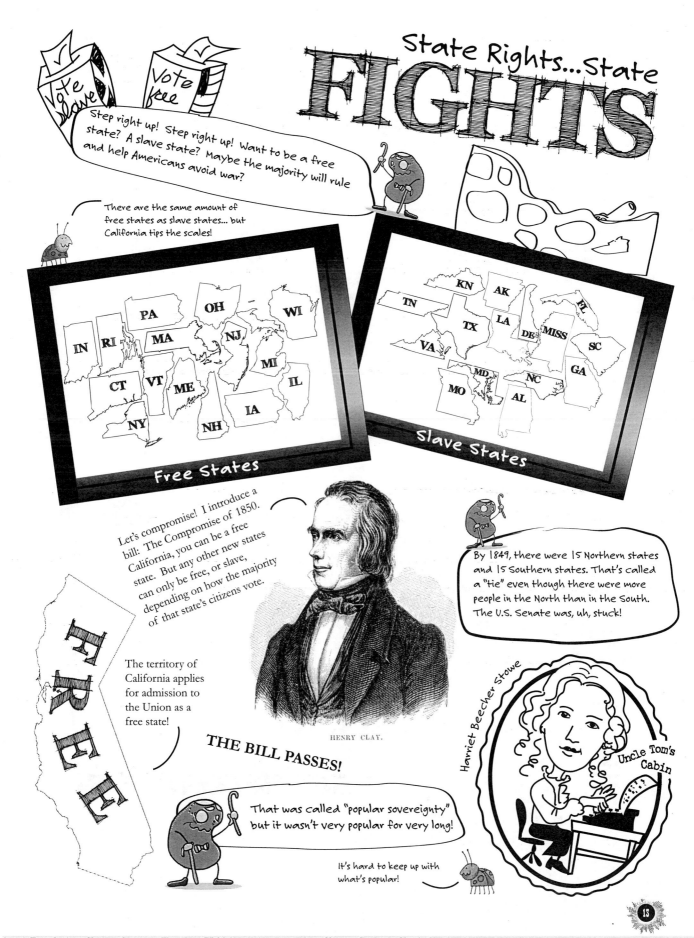

State Rights...State
FIGHTS

Step right up! Step right up! Want to be a free state? A slave state? Maybe the majority will rule and help Americans avoid war?

There are the same amount of free states as slave states... but California tips the scales!

Free States

PA OH WI
IN RI MA NJ
CT VT ME MI IL
NY NH IA

Slave States

KN AK FL
TN LA DE MISS
TX VA SC
MO MD NC GA
AL

Let's compromise! I introduce a bill: The Compromise of 1850. California, you can be a free state. But any other new states can only be free, or slave, depending on how the majority of that state's citizens vote.

By 1849, there were 15 Northern states and 15 Southern states. That's called a "tie" even though there were more people in the North than in the South. The U.S. Senate was, uh, stuck!

FREE

The territory of California applies for admission to the Union as a free state!

HENRY CLAY.

THE BILL PASSES!

Harriet Beecher Stowe

Uncle Tom's Cabin

That was called "popular sovereignty" but it wasn't very popular for very long!

It's hard to keep up with what's popular!

13

forms Female Anti-Slavery Society...Theodore Weld forms American Anti-Slavery Society...Ohio's Oberlin College 1st to admit blacks...1835... South Carolina

people organize to press their demands for justice... President Roosevelt issues an executive order against discrimination of workers in defense industries and government...1942... Margaret Walker wins the Yale Award for Young Poets for her

Fruit Basket

TURN OVER

By 1852, America was a zoo of activity and emotions!

Settlers, pioneers, homesteaders, and frontiersmen push West, push out Native Americans, and push for states' rights!

Oof!

Make room! Make room! States coming through!

uh oh

New president Franklin Pierce lost in the "gathering storm" of war talk!

Hit 'im with your left! Your other left!

Missouri Compromise gets uncompromised…abolitionists and Free-Soilers furious…Kansas-Nebraska Act creates two new huge territories, risking the spread of slavery!

I don't think I like the forecast!

Stephen A. Douglas pushes for a transcontinental railroad…Republican political party is born…angry skirmishes in "Bleeding Kansas"… a free-for-all fist fight in Congress puts Americans in an even more warlike, angry mood!

14

burns abolitionist literature…Georgia threatens to enact death penalty for abolitionist writers…Abolitionist William Ellery Channing publishes Slavery…1836

moving collection of poems, "For My People"…1947…Lawyer and economist, Sadie T.M. Alexander is appointed to Truman's Commission on Civil Rights…CORE sends its first group of "Freedom Riders" through the South…1948… President

Recipes for DISASTER!

A couple of dreadful events set the stage for war!

RECIPE

Dred Scott in a Pot

Was the slave, Dred Scott, entitled to be free because he had lived for several years in the free lands of the North? In 1857, the U.S. Supreme Court said, "No!" The court ruled that slaves were "property" and no matter where they went, they were still slaves. This did not please Northerners, Southerners, or, as you might imagine, slaves.

Simmer all this discontent well and watch the pot boil! Serves: no one

Boy, this is some mess!

RECIPE

John Brown failed at business and farming. He excelled at causing trouble. As an abolitionist in Kansas Territory, he went unpunished for the murder of five people. Next, he and some buddies sneaked into Harpers Ferry, Virginia and took over the federal arsenal of weapons in a plan to lead slaves to rebel against their masters to achieve freedom. After four people were killed, troops stormed the arsenal. John Brown was wounded and taken prisoner. He was hanged for murder and treason.

Northerners thought Brown was a hero. Southerners thought the "John Browns" of the North would continue to do such lawless things, and so they began to gather groups of soldiers "just in case" a war was coming.

Add the spices of years of disagreement, hatred, raw emotions, passion for a cause, desperation, and fear.

Bake at a hot temperature. Leave the room or leave the Union…wait for the explosion!

…Arkansas joins Union as slave state…1837…Michigan joins Union as free state…1845…Florida joins Union as slave state…Texas joins union as slave state

Truman issues an executive order banning segregation in the armed forces…Pharmacist Ella Nora Phillips Stewart is elected president of the National Association of Colored Women…Edith Irby Jones is the first black to be admitted to a Southern

"THANKS but no thanks!"

South Carolina 1860

We will not accept this determination to end slavery and our Southern way of life.

We vote for an "ordinance of seccession," which means our state is leaving the United States to go it alone!

The Confederacy has 7 states now! Alabama, Florida, Georgia, Louisiana, Mississippi, South Carolina and Texas.

Other states also leave the Union. We all went to Montgomery, Alabama and formed our own government—the Confederate States of America!

AL
MISS
LA
FL
GA

Before he was the President, Abe was a lawyer, a Representative, and even ran for Senate! Wow!

Well, I finally get elected president only to have my country split into two parts. But no state has the right to leave the Union just because it wants to! That's illegal!

- Abraham Lincoln

I am the president of the Confederacy. We just aren't going to put up with being pushed around! Our militia is taking over federal posts that are located in our new "country." Many are laying down their weapons without even a fight!

- Jefferson Davis

But not all...

...1848...Wisconsin joins Union as free state...Treaty of Guadalupe Hidalgo signed ending Mexican War—U.S. gains Texas, California, and all land in between...

medical school, The University of Arkansas...1954...In the Brown vs. Board of Education Case, the U.S. Supreme Court declares segregation in public schools unconstitutional...1955...The U.S. Supreme Court orders school integration "with all

READY, FIRE, AIM!

The U.S. troops at Fort Sumter in South Carolina refused to surrender to the Confederate soldiers. But the Confederate soldiers were determined to take the fort. They mounted cannons on the beaches on three sides of the fort, and on April 12, 1861 opened fire! The Union soldiers just watched for 36 hours, then surrendered. The fort was now a useless heap of bricks, and no one was really hurt. But this was a...CLEAR ACT OF WAR! The Civil War—the "War Between the States" had begun!

RECIPE

War Casserole

Ingredients:
1 nation broken into 2 parts
gobs of hot tempers
a hefty sprinkling of stubbornness
a real hankerin' for a fight
1 place: Fort Sumter
2 wads of soldiers, squared off
1 call to "Open fire!"

Fire in the hole!

They were between a rock and a hard place!

They sure were!

We all had to choose—North or South? Some of us were squeezed in between—which neighbors did we side with? Did we pick to support our Union, or did we join the Confederacy?

Mississippi, Florida, Alabama, Georgia, Lousiana and Texas left the Union. Kentucky chose to be "neutral." Maryland and Missouri stayed in the Union.

AK

NC

TN

VA

17

1850...Congress passes the Compromise of 1850...1852...Harriet Beecher Stowe publishes Uncle Tom's Cabin...1854...Congress passes the Kansas-Nebraska

deliberate speed."...In Montgomery, Alabama, Rosa Parks refuses to give up her seat on a public bus to a white man. She is arrested and jailed...A year-long bus boycott results in the U.S. Supreme Court invalidating segregation on Montgomery

A War By Any Other Name is Still a...

WAR!

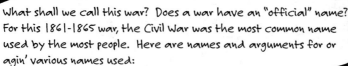

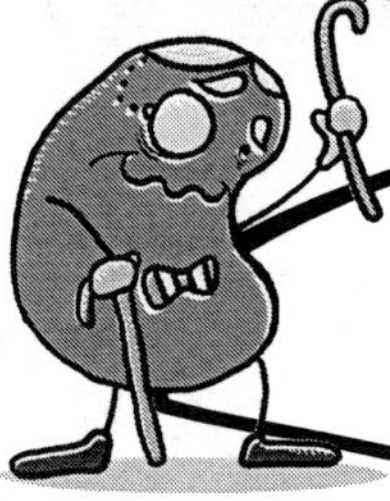

What shall we call this war? Does a war have an "official" name? For this 1861-1865 war, the Civil War was the most common name used by the most people. Here are names and arguments for or agin' various names used:

NAME

What would you have called the Civil War?

1) Civil War
2) War Between the States
3) War of the Rebellion

4) War for Southern Independence
5) Second American Revolution
6) The War for Nationality

7) War of Secession
8) The War Against Slavery
9) War of Separation

10) Conflict of the Sixties
11) The War for the Union
12) The Confederate War

13) Mr. Lincoln's War
14) The Uncivil War
15) The Brothers' War

16) War Against the States
17) The Lost Cause
18) The War

19) The Yankee Invasion
20) The Southern Defense Against Northern Aggression
21) The Late Unpleasantness

BUT SOME SAY...

1) But we aren't fighting to control a single government!
2) But that makes it sound like its not about slavery!
3) Well, why do you think they call us Rebels, you all?

4) It's just like being a colonist again!
5) Wasn't the first one enough?
6) Huh?

7) But sess...secc...secession's too hard to spell!
8) I vote for that!
9) Yeah, I was separated from my family four long years!

10) Wasn't that the Battle of Woodstock?
11) How many names do there really need to be for one war?
12) Hey, we didn't fight this thing by ourselves!

13) Why blame him?
14) Finally, something we all can agree on!
15) Too sad.

16) Huh?
17) I think it got found—check the number of books on this subject!
18) Duh?

19) Take that, ya'll!
20) Too long! Too long!
21) Well, that's what Auntie Bellum called it...

¹⁸

Act...1856...Proslavery candidate James Buchanan elected president...1857...Supreme Court rules escaped slave Dred Scott is property that must be returned

buses...1957...As president of the state NAACP, Daisy Gatson Bates leads the fight for school integration in Little Rock, Arkansas...1960...First student sit-ins at a lunch counter in Greensboro, North Carolina...1961...More than 50,000 people

The Civil War in a Nutshell...

In 1619 slaves were brought to America. *Hey, how come we have to be the slaves? Not sure, sorry.* Plantation owners in the South used slaves to grow crops like cotton. *Hey, Eli, hurry up and invent the cotton gin! Who's asking? Boll, Boll Weevil.* People in the North didn't grow many crops, they made things. *Like what?* Like shoes, clothes, railroads and things. *So they didn't need slaves?* No. Some thought slavery was wrong. They said so. *Abolitionists?* Yes. The South ignored them, said they'd always had slaves, and needed them. *Everyone in the South owned slaves?* No, very few did. *Everyone in the North opposed slavery?* No, but lots did. Americans also argued over whether the federal government...*That's Washington, DC, right?* Yes...or each state should have the most powerful laws. *Like about slavery?* Like about slavery.

> This was a big nut to crack.

New states joined as Free states or Slave states. Senator Henry Clay made a compromise law so states could decide for themselves. Some people didn't like this and kept fighting over whether slavery was right or wrong. John Brown tried to lead a slave revolt. It didn't work. He was hanged for breaking the law. But people couldn't forget him. In 1860 Abraham Lincoln was elected president. Abe was against slavery and everybody knew it. That made some people happy and others UNhappy. That same year, South Carolina said, "We don't wanna be part of the United States of America anymore!" Other states also seceded. *How could they do that?* They just did, even though it was illegal. Abe had a problem. The country was dividing into pieces. Georgia, Louisiana, Florida, South Carolina, Alabama, Mississippi, Virginia, Texas, Arkansas, North Carolina, and Tennessee became the Confederate States of America under the leadership of Jefferson Davis. They made their own flag. *The Rebel flag, right?* Right, and their own government. That very year, Confederates-some called 'em Rebels-and the Union-some called 'em Yanks-met up at Fort Sumter in South Carolina. With one shot **BOOM!** the Civil War officially began! No one was killed but it excited lots of people. Soldiers came from everywhere! Boys, men, teenagers, grandpas, fathers, sons, brothers, uncles, even some girls *wanted* to fight. Soldiers picked their side-North or South-and joined the army. The first battle was at Bull Run, or Manassas, depending on whether you're a Yankee or Southerner. Confederates won, hands down. Next came battle after battle. There was a battle between two iron ships, the *Monitor* and the *Merrimac.* Then Battle of Shiloh, Seven Days Battle, Second Battle of Bull Run, and Battle of Antietam, bloodiest of the Civil War. There were soldiers fighting battles all over. While one was happening on a field in Virginia, another was happening by a creek in Alabama. There were too many to count! In 1863, Lincoln issued the Emancipation Proclamation. It said all slaves were free. The slaves *loved* it, the North *loved* it, the South *hated* it! Fighting continued in Chancellorsville, Tennessee. General Stonewall Jackson was hit **POW!** He died a few days later. Soldiers fought a bloody battle at Gettysburg, Pennsylvania. Thousands died on both sides. But the Union said they won. The Union had been losing most battles and wanted to quit. But Gettysburg revived their spirits. They fought in Vicksburg, Mississippi, such a long battle people ate rats! *Ewww!* And Chickamauga. On November 19, 1863, President Lincoln gave the Gettysburg Address and said "all men are created equal." *Even slaves?* Especially slaves. The South still didn't agree. The Civil War kept going. General Ulysses S. Grant became head of the Union army. He led troops through the Battle of the Wilderness and finally to Petersburg Virginia. The Union backed the Confederates into a corner. It was...quiet...no...gunshots...cannons... or fighting. Soldiers stared at each other...waiting...waiting...waiting for someone to make a move. While those soldiers waited in Virginia, other Confederates tried to protect Atlanta, Georgia from the Yankees. General William T. Sherman led Union soldiers toward Atlanta. The Rebels *PUSHHHEEEDDD* against Sherman. Sherman *PUSHHHEEEDDD* against the Rebels. Sherman won. He burned Atlanta to the ground! Then he *walked* through almost the whole state with his entire army. He ended up in Savannah, Georgia, which he "gave" to President Lincoln as a Christmas gift! Back in Petersburg, those soldiers were *still* staring at each other until the Confederates tried to protect an important railroad station.

> I'm shellshocked!

> I'm crushed, just crushed.

They failed. They marched to Richmond, Virginia with the Union on their heels. Richmond was the Confederate States of America's capital. The soldiers, led by General Robert E. Lee, did all they could to protect Richmond. They failed. They kept marching backwards, slowly running from the Union. The Confederates ended up at Appomattox Court House, Virginia. Robert E. Lee had nowhere to turn. He didn't want more men to die. He surrendered. Lee and Grant met. Lee signed surrender papers. Grant said Lee was dignified and took defeat gracefully. *So the war was over?* Yes, officially, but some battles continued until the word got around. By the time the four year war was over, more than 618,000 men had died. It took years to rebuild the South and help the slaves learn how to be free. But the United States was one nation again. *What did the soldiers do?* They went home.

Civil War Generals Collectible Cards

"A Motley Crew, Yet Magnificent!"

I'll trade my Jackson for your Grant!

Deal!

A Helpful Index
- Cannons for power
- Medals for legacy
- Brains for smarts
- Flags for defense
- Fear for cowardice

Abraham Lincoln
He didn't fight but He *was* powerful!   5x

Union

Fashionista Rating: ☆
For bad beard and overall strange look
Positives: ✓ ✓ ✓ ✓
Helped end slavery
Special Skills: ❗❗❗❗
Convincing speaker, confident leader
Post War Stats: A++
One of America's greatest presidents

Jefferson Davis
Not quite as strong as Abe, but something to watch out for!   4x

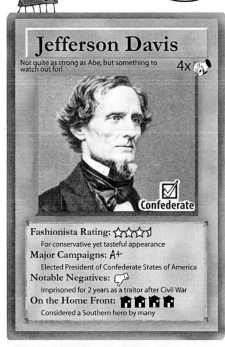
Confederate

Fashionista Rating: ☆☆☆☆
For conservative yet tasteful appearance
Major Campaigns: A+
Elected President of Confederate States of America
Notable Negatives: 👎
Imprisoned for 2 years as a traitor after Civil War
On the Home Front: 🏠🏠🏠🏠
Considered a Southern hero by many

Robert E. Lee
The Confederates' most powerful general!   4.5x

Confederate

Fashionista Rating: ☆☆☆☆☆
One word: Classy!
Defense Points: 🚩🚩🚩🚩🚩
For fighting outnumbered and still winning!
Notable Negatives: 👎👎👎
Forced to surrender the Confederate Army to U.S. Grant
Serious Smarts: 🧠🧠🧠🧠🧠
Outsmarted even the strongest Union Generals

Thomas "Stonewall" Jackson
He never lived up to his full power potential   3x

Confederate

Fashionista Rating: ☆☆☆☆☆ / ☆
Pre beard / post beard
Injuries: ➕➕➕➕➕
Gunshot to the shoulder during battle, +1 for losing an arm
Special Effects: ⚡⚡⚡
Ability to stand strong, like a stone wall, in the face of danger
Legendary Legacy: 🏅🏅🏅🏅🏅
Honored by North and South

P.G.T. Beauregard
For his French name!   2.5x ♥

Confederate

Fashionista Rating: ☆☆☆☆☆
For having 3 initials!
Likeability: D+
Did not get along with President Jefferson Davis
On the Home Front: 🏠🏠🏠🏠
National hero in his home state, Louisiana
Post War Stats: B-
Important Louisiana politician

Ulysses S. Grant
Union's most powerful general, just strong enough to win!   5x

Union

Fashionista Rating: 👎
For appearance negligence
Attack Points: 🔫🔫🔫🔫🔫
For attacking until the Confederates couldn't fight back
Legendary Legacy: 🏅🏅🏅🏅
Honored as one of the greatest generals of the Civil War
Post War Stats: A
Became president of United States in 1869

J.E.B. Stuart
Charming and gallant!   3x ♥

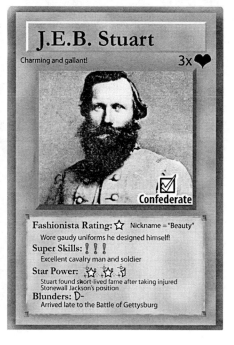
Confederate

Fashionista Rating: ☆ Nickname = "Beauty"
Wore gaudy uniforms he designed himself!
Super Skills: ❗❗❗
Excellent cavalry man and soldier
Star Power: ☆☆☆
Stuart found short-lived fame after taking injured Stonewall Jackson's position
Blunders: D-
Arrived late to the Battle of Gettysburg

Nathan Bedford Forrest

A military genius!   5x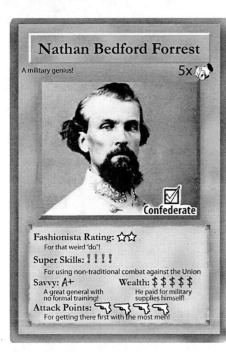

Confederate

Fashionista Rating: ⭐⭐☆
For that weird "do"!

Super Skills: ❗❗❗❗
For using non-traditional combat against the Union

Savvy: A+
A great general with no formal training!

Wealth: $ $ $ $ $
He paid for military supplies himself!

Attack Points: 🐾🐾🐾🐾🐾
For getting there first with the most men!

Joseph E. Johnston

Did he lack the will to win?   1x

Confederate

Injuries: ✚✚✚✚
Was replaced by Robert E. Lee after an injury in battle

Likeability: C+
Had conflict with Jefferson Davis

Special Effects: ⚡⚡⚡⚡
Slowed Sherman's Army from reaching Atlanta

Legendary Legacy: 🐻🐻🐻🐻
Some said he was a better general than Robert E. Lee!

Ambrose Burnside

West Point grad!   1.5x

Union

Fashionista Rating: -☆
For those ugly sideburns!

Noteable Negatives: 👎👎👎👎
Failed commander of the Army of the Potomac

Serious Smarts: 🧠🧠🧠
For trying to admit his inexperience to the U.S. government

Fated Follies: C-
Put on leave from Union Army and never called back to serve

William T. Sherman

For burning Atlanta!   6x

Union

Fashionista Rating: ⭐⭐
Too intimidating!

Attack Points: 🐾🐾🐾🐾
For conquering Atlanta and the March to the Sea

Cruel Intentions: 😠😠😠😠
For plundering innocent Confederate property

Legendary Legacy: 🐻
Remembered in the South as a cruel Union general

George McClellan

Hated to fight!   -10x

Union

Fashionista Rating: ⭐⭐⭐⭐
Out of date mustache

Fear Factor: 😨😨😨😨😨😨😨😨😨
He was sort of cowardly!

Attack Points: ∅
For skittish fighting with the Army of the Potomac

Post War Stats: F-
Remembered as an unsuccessful general and presidential candidate

John Lincoln "Johnny" Clem

Drummer boy!   6x ♪

Union

Fashionista Rating: ⭐⭐⭐⭐⭐
For cuteness

Bravery: A++
For being a 9-year-old soldier!

Special Effects: ⚡⚡⚡
For playing a mean drum!

Luck: High
For surviving multiple bullet shots

Post War Stats: A
Became a major general in the army

Traveller the Horse

He carried Robert E. Lee, the South's greatest general   5x

Confederate

Fashionista Rating: ⭐⭐⭐⭐⭐
A noble steed

Star Power: ⭐⭐⭐⭐⭐
Most famous horse of the Civil War

Legendary Legacy: 🐻🐻🐻🐻🐻
He now rests next to Robert E. Lee at Washington and Lee University

Frederick Douglass

Recruited black soldiers for the North   4x

Union

Fashionista Rating: ⭐⭐⭐
That bowtie rocks!

Bravery: A+
For escaping from slavery!

Serious Smarts: 🧠🧠🧠🧠
For educating himself!

Legendary Legacy: 🐻🐻🐻🐻
For being a leader in African American civil rights!

Harriet Tubman

Led hundreds of slaves to freedom on the Underground Railroad   5x ♥

Union

Fashionista Rating: ⭐⭐
For not smiling

Positives: ✓✓✓✓
In the abolitionist movement

Stealth: A+
For smuggling slaves to freedom, and never getting caught!

Legendary Legacy: 🐻🐻🐻🐻🐻
For being a leader in civil rights and women's rights

Invitation to a WAR

And so, the Civil War was underway. It might be hard for us to imagine today, but most people thought that this war would be...

And OUR side will win!

Short! Easy!

Few deaths; not much bloodshed!

But nothing beats the women who packed up a picnic and came to "enjoy" watching the first real battle just outside Washington, D.C.!

The South is uh, this way? This way?

The immediate problem was that in spite of years of arguing, neither the North nor the South were ready to fight a war! Here were some of the problems:

- General-in-Chief of the U.S. Army, Winfield Scott, was older than dirt!
- America's "army" was made up of only 16,000 men, all spread out across 3 million square miles in 140 different forts and outposts!
- The Army was very old-fashioned and outmoded.
- So was the War Department!
- Everything was very disorganized!
- They didn't have accurate maps!

Seen a soldier?

Uh, not lately.

At least the North had a White House, Congress, a capitol building (which had no roof!), a flag, records, a post office system, courts, and such—but many of the people who knew how to lead or run them left to fight for the South! Poor President Lincoln!

In the South, they had no head start for war! The Confederacy was just a baby "country" with no constitution, or much of anything else—especially no army.

Strategy? Strategy? Hmm...what's that?

And then there was that problem called "strategy." Was WAS their strategy?

19

to owner...1858...Minnesota joins Union as free state...Illinois candidates Abraham Lincoln and Stephen Douglas debate issues of slavery; Douglas wins

demonstrate for equal rights in 100 cities, and over 3,600 are jailed...1963...Dr. Martin Luther King, Jr., delivers his "I Have a Dream" speech...Gloria Richardson is the only black woman to lead a local civil rights group... Charlayne Hunter-Gault is

S is for Strategy!

At the start of the war, it was hard to see what our strategies were! See what you think!

The Civil War was all about strategy—when there was one! In any war lots of decisions are made, good and bad. Some good ones still lead to disaster. Some bad ones can turn to victory. Some are made long ahead, others on the spur of the moment. Some generals are great strategists, others, well, not so much so!

I'll stick to eating dirt, thanks!

Strategy sure looks hard!

Good?   Bad?

Strategy

Confederates move the South's capital from Montgomery, Alabama (far from Washington!) to "across the street" from Washington, in Richmond, Virginia.

> Both! The capital was near where the fighting was.

The South's 11 farming states try to compete at war with 23 Northern states of cities, seaports, fields, and factories*.

> Bad! Not so smart!

When the South signed up soldiers for the war, they took these men away from productive jobs that produced food and supplies for the war.

> Not so good; Southern soldiers went hungry.

The South had more and better military schools so they had stronger military leaders.

> Great! Generals like Robert E. Lee and Stonewall Jackson!

The North chose generals who'd been working in stores, on the railroad or streetcars.

> Bad, but Gen. Grant learned fast!

The North had more war "stuff."

> Lots more! Great for the North!

The South had little money.

> Very little. Bad for the South!

The South had much more land to guard and protect.

> But they had obstacles like mountain ranges, which was good!

The North was close to the major battle areas.

> But it was full of forests, creeks, and Confederates! Very bad!

*That was 22,000,000 Northerners vs. 5,500,000 Southerners (slaves not counted), or about 2 million Union soldiers vs. 800,000 Rebels.

election to Senate…1859…Oregon joins Union as free state…Abolitionist John Brown leads slave revolt; Brown is hanged…1860…Antislavery candidate

the first black woman to receive a degree from the University of Georgia…1964… Fannie Lou Hamer is a founder and vice chairperson of the Mississippi Freedom Democratic Party…1964…The Civil Rights Act prohibits discrimination in public

So, What Was the War About Now?

The plot thickens!

Good question! Once war began, the North's main goal was to force the South back into the Union. That meant they had to attack and move their soldiers through dense forests toward the Confederate enemy ready and waiting for them at their defensive positions. It is said that it takes three soldiers to successfully attack one soldier defending. That meant that in spite of the North having more soldiers, the odds were now much more even. Also the Southerners got to stay in territory they were familiar with. The Union soldiers were on new terrain. The plot thickened!

Come and get me, Yankees!

Push 'em back, push 'em back, Push 'em waaaay back!

Monday Morning Quarterbacking with the Generals!

Defense! Defense!

We thought we could just wait for you Yankees to get tired and quit and go home.

We were afraid you would win. You know, just never give up. Unless the Union was like a 100%, it would always be like a loss to us.

What if we had known what we were getting ourselves into, what might we have done differently?

Too late for that!

Oh, well there's always another war!

Let's hope not!

Got to go stir the plot!

Abraham Lincoln elected president…South Carolina votes to secede from the Union…1861…Florida, Alabama, Georgia, Mississippi, and Louisiana secede from

facilities; in employment on the basis of sex, religion, nationality; and establishes the Equal Employment Opportunity Commission… Lawyer, Marion Wright Edelman establishes the NAACP's Legal Defense and Education Fund Office in Jackson,

It Was Just One You-Know-What Battle After
ANOTHER!

Alas, war finally boils down to fighting, bloodshed, and death, only no one expected four long years of that or just how very, very bad it would be!

The Major Battles of the Civil War…
not including scads of smaller skirmishes!

BATTLE	WHERE	WIN/LOSE/DRAW
1st Manassas/ 1st Bull Run	Virginia	Union defeated
Shiloh	Tennessee	Rebel troops retreat
Seven Days	Virginia	Army of the Potomac retreats
2nd Manassas/ 2nd Bull Run	Virginia	Union defeated again
Antietam	Maryland	A losing proposition for all
Chancellorsville	The Wilderness	Gen. Lee's greatest victory
Vicksburg	Mississippi	Gen. Grant wins
Gettysburg	Pennsylvania	Turns the tide of war
Chattanooga	Tennessee	Confederates lose out
The Wilderness	Virginia	No ground gained on either side
Atlanta Campaign	Georgia	The city is burned!
"March to the Sea"	Georgia	Sherman gives Savannah to President Lincoln for Christmas
Franklin	Tennessee	Confederates lose

That Gen. Grant was tough!

Take that, Yanks!

Bloodiest single day of the whole war!

Can't win 'em all…

Don't give Gen. Sherman any more matches!

Not very merry for us.

It was a bad way to start.

We gotta stop meeting like this!

That darn Stonewall Jackson!

We Yanks pull ahead!

Five generals killed!

And this was not all the battles. Don't forget Cedar Creek, Chickamauga, Cold Harbor, Fort Henry and Fort Donelson, Fredericksburg, Murfreesboro, Pea Ridge, Perryville, Petersburg, Sayler's Creek, Spotsylvania, Stone's River, Winchester, and many more.

Union…Kansas joins Union as free state…Southern states form Confederate States of America…Jefferson Davis elected Confederate president…Richmond

Mississippi…1965…Septima Poinsette Clark leads an Southern Christian Leadership Conference group which registers about 7,000 black voters in Alabama…Voting Rights Act allows blacks to vote freely and unhindered…1966… Black Panther

Virginia is named capital of the Confederate States of America…Texas secedes; joins Confederacy…South Carolina troops attack Federal Fort Sumter…Civil War

Party forms to establish black power in America…1967… President Lyndon B. Johnson appoints the first black U.S. Supreme Court Justice, Thurgood Marshall…1968…Dr. Martin Luther King, Jr., is assassinated in Memphis, Tennessee…New

What was an "ARMY" Made Up of, Anyway?

That's a lot of mouths to feed!

When I joined up, I was put in a 100 man "company." A captain and lieutenant were in charge.

Passion, patriotism, and "fightin' words" sent many men rushing to join their army. But let Joe tell how it worked for him.

10 companies were banded into a "regiment," led by a colonel.

5 regiments made a "brigade" under a brigadier general. Regiments had names like the 18th Virginia or 101st Pennsylvania.

3-5 brigades made a division.

3-5 divisions made a corps.

● = **COMPANY** (100 men)

● = **REGIMENT** (1,000 men)

= **BRIGADE** (5,000 men)

= **DIVISION** (15,000 men)

= **CORPS** (45,000 men)

And all of us altogether made an army!

Unknown Soldier 1862

Sickness, desertion, wounds, and death quickly reduced most armies by drastic numbers!

officially begins...Federal Navy blockades Southern ports...Virginia, Arkansas, North Carolina, and Tennessee join Confederacy...Union defeated at Battle of

York elects Shirley Chisholm as first African American U.S. Congresswoman...1969...Mary Moultrie leads a wage strike at the Medical College Hospital in South Carolina...1972...Political activist and intellectual, Angela Davis is acquitted of murder

New TOOLS

Since the Civil War lasted four long years, there was time for ingenuity, improvements, inventions, and new ideas to affect how things were done.

Whatever it's called, I like it!

Cotton gin is short for "cotton engine."

Eli Whitney invented the cotton gin which meant less slave labor was required.

The rifle was invented, which meant soldiers didn't have to stand around vulnerable while they reloaded the long, heavy Springfield musket. They could fire more shots and hit more targets.

Bullseye!

Other things invented during the war:
machine gun • hand grenade • land mines • ironclad ships • telegraph communication in war • railroads for military transportation • "drafting" men into armies • a wagon "ambulance" to transport wounded soldiers • manned observation balloons • the first African American troops • more than 2,000 Civil War songs • paper money • tax collection • left and right-footed shoes • flowers for funerals • the Congressional Medal of Honor • the American Red Cross • Santa Claus • the bugle call "Taps"

Bull Run—first official battle of the Civil War...1862...1st ironclad ship battle between Monitor and Merrimac...2nd Battle of Bull Run ends in Union defeat

in a political trial in California... Equal Employment Opportunity Act passes...1974...The Coalition of Labor Union Women is formed...1978...U.S. Postal Service issues a Black Heritage postage stamp series...1983...Martin Luther King, Jr. Day is

What About the GUTS?

President Lincoln had guts. He was elected at a treacherous and confusing crossroads in American history. Jefferson Davis, president of the Confederacy, had guts to take on the role as leader of a bunch of rebellious states determined to fight to the death for what they believed in. These presumably arch-enemies had a lot in common:

There were all kind of "guts."

Born in Kentucky

Tall and thin

Serious thinkers

Almost the same age

Elected to office on the eve of war

Read a lot

Good public speakers

Loved their country

Devoted patriots

And yet, Lincoln is considered the greatest president America ever had. Davis was considered a failure.

Why? Perhaps because one had the right talents and timing for the Civil War. The other was eventually overwhelmed by the responsibilities and obstacles of war. Yet both were great men, beloved, and had what we call "guts."

Having "guts" was exhibited in all sorts of valiant and foolish ways. From the wife who dodged bullets to bring her husband soldier a sandwich…to spies who risked their lives to get information to share with their leaders…to nurses and doctors who tried to help the wounded and dying, even as a battle roared around them…there were many heroes in the Civil War. Most never expected to be heroes. All surely would have traded that fame just to be home safe with their loved ones, at peace.

Hurry home please, darling!

…Battle of Antietam becomes bloodiest day of the Civil War…1st black regiment formed…1863…President Lincoln issues Emancipation Proclamation…Union

first celebrated on January 20th as a federal holiday...1989…General Colin Powell chosen as first black chairman of Joint Chiefs of Staff, the nation's top military position…1991… Civil Rights Act limits affirmative action…1992…Mae Jemison

"No Guts, No GLORY!"

Not only was the Civil War fraught with danger, it was extremely bloody! Generals and privates died from blood loss due to wounds or amputations. What didn't kill them outright often did soon enough, from infections to disease. Indeed, sickness was the greatest killer in the war. Germs were more deadly than bullets! For every man killed in battle, two died of illness. At any given time, half of either army was too ill to fight. Remember there were no immunizations against childhood (or any other) diseases, and men crowded on battlefields and in living quarters gave and got diseases.

What killed most soldiers? DIARRHEA!

This isn't what I signed up for!

Those musket balls were so soft they just sorta squashed their way through a body, leaving a big, gashing hole, and tearing up all the flesh in their path.

The nurse said I had gangrene. She wept. I didn't know what she meant then, but as I lay alone in the woods, stinking and dying my horrid death, I learned.

The doc put me on an old door on the ground and gave me a swig of whiskey. "Bite down on this," he said, and thrust a stick between my teeth. Then he cut off my leg with a rusty knife. It took 10 minutes but felt like 10 years.

As if all this was not bad enough, exposure to weather, rotted food, contaminated water, filth, no medications, few doctors, and medical "expertise" that was still in the Dark Ages—all contributed to death galore. The heartbreak of war is unimaginable. There were men with plenty of guts...who never stood a chance of getting out of the war alive.

27

War Department establishes Bureau of Colored Troops...Confederate General Thomas "Stonewall" Jackson killed... Grant conquers Vicksburg, Mississippi

becomes the first African American female U.S. astronaut...1993...Toni Morrison becomes first African American female to win a Pulitzer Prize in literature for her novel, Beloved...2000...President George W. Bush appoints African American

Who Won? Who LOST?

Lee surrenders at Appomattox Court House

What exactly was "winning" or "losing" in a war like this?

The history books tell us that Gen. Lee "surrendered" to Gen. Grant at Appomattox Courthouse, Virginia on April 9, 1865. Perhaps surprisingly to us, this was a calm, quiet ceremony, where the "losers" were honored with respect and grace. Why don't you judge for yourselves, who won and who lost.

Although the South "surrendered," the North, too, had lost leaders, youth, men with skills, and all the work, talent, and families they might have contributed to the future. The death toll was: **618,000**

President Lincoln was assassinated on April 14, leaving the reunited nation without their heroic leader.

Wounded, exhausted, or otherwise "broken" men walked long ways back home, and were greeted with burned towns, destroyed crops, and no idea how to mend their world and their lives.

EMANCIPATION PROCLAMATION

The 1863 Emancipation Proclamation had freed slaves. But freedom was frightening and fraught with peril. The North did not welcome freed blacks and those who remained in the South were often at a loss of how to survive now that they did not have anyone to look after any of their needs.

The period after the war known as Reconstruction was a hard time of bitterness, corruption, and great disappointment, especially in the war-torn South.

On the "winning" side, America was now one nation again. Amendments to the U.S. Constitution meant that slavery was a thing of the past, and that equality was truly the right of all Americans. Of course, as we know, the "war" for equality in voting rights for blacks and women, and justice for all was still to be fought during the Civil Rights years and beyond.

In spite of the eternal great wish that war could have been avoided, America and Americans proved that they could overcome such a devastating milestone in their history and go on to create an ever greater nation devoted to peace, prosperity, and a fair future for all.

...Union gains control of Mississippi River...West Virginia joins Union as free state...Battle of Gettysburg begins to turn tide of war for Union... Lincoln gives

Condoleezza Rice to serve as his U.S. National Security Advisor...2002...Tiger Woods becomes the youngest golfer (age 26!) to win 8 PGA major titles... African American tennis star Serena Williams wins the U.S. Open and Wimbledon

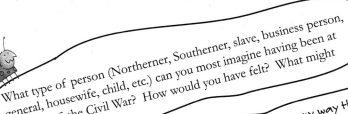

QUESTIONS

for Discussion

What type of person (Northerner, Southerner, slave, business person, general, housewife, child, etc.) can you most imagine having been at the start of the Civil War? How would you have felt? What might you have done?

Do you see any way that the Civil War might have been avoided? If so, how could that have changed history? If not, what does that say about how we continue to "get into" wars today?

Who were the "good guys" or heroes in the Civil War, in your mind? Who were the "bad guys" or those who helped make things even worse than they were?

Was anyone in America at that time unaffected by the Civil War?

What is the difference between fighting a war in some other country, versus having war fought in your own homeland?

Who were the "winners" or "losers" in the Civil War, in your mind?

What can we learn from the Civil War that we can apply to federal, state, local, and personal actions and behaviors today?

How do we know when going to war is essential versus when diplomacy, compromise, or some other solution would work instead of fighting?

How differently do you think the following people might feel about war: president; politician; business person; wife; mother; child; soldier; boy almost of military age?

What do we think, and what are our ideas, when we see "civil wars" being fought in other countries today?

Gettysburg Address…Union forces gain control Tennessee…1864…Grant appointed commander of Union Army…General Sherman conquers Atlanta, Georgia

tournaments…Talk show host Oprah Winfery receives the first Bob Hope Humanitarian Award at the 54th Annual Emmy Awards…Halle Berry becomes first African American to win an Academy Award for best actress…The Slavery Reparations

OR, WHAT Historians Say Today...
How Come We're Still Fightin' This Dang War?!

This is a dangerous page for me to write! Why? Because, believe it or not, even though the Civil War happened 150 years ago, people are still "fighting" the war. Mostly, this is a war of words, but important words.

We always want to know the "truth," but truth is often elusive and, as is said, in the eye of the beholder. Some people just have opinions. These might be correct, or they might be something they have just read or heard others say, true or not. Some people are "experts," but they might still be biased or prejudiced in some ways. Some "truths" were right, but new information can require some clarification...sometimes even a total upheaval of what we once "believed" to be true.

Confusing? Yes, but it's also what makes history so dynamic and fascinating.

Here are just a few of the Civil War interpretations still under discussion. Why should you care? Because you will read or hear about some of these in the news most everyday!

Truth in history. This certainly affects school students! If you live in one part of the country, perhaps your textbooks say one thing; in another part of the country, perhaps something different. Even if only slightly different, it makes a difference. Location, opinions, the "times" we live in, historic interpretations, and even bias and prejudice can affect what is said to be the "truth." *Interesting, huh?*

Wow, I didn't know I had to work so hard at this?

Those poignant Civil War historic sites. Some people think that they should be preserved and protected, and not encroached upon by nearby shopping malls, theme parks, subdivisions, or anything else that diminishes the surrounding views that distract from the battlefields or parks. Other people think progress means we build what we want or need on available land. *What do you think?*

That doggone Confederate flag! Some people believe that the Confederate battle flag is part of history, that it represented the pride and spirit of the Confederate troops. Other people claim that the Confederate flag implies that slavery was good, and when flown today, is obnoxious and insulting. *What do you think?*

Well you do if you don't want to be a history ignoramus!

Reparations for slavery. Even after all these years, some people believe that there should be formal apologies to people who had slaves in their families, and perhaps even monetary reparations (cold, hard cash!) for lost land or opportunities or rights. *How do you feel?*

And if you want to be a good citizen!

Uh, let's go play some ball, ok?

Federal rights versus states' rights. This is a real conundrum. Whether it's health care or protecting our borders, states often argue with one another, as well as with the federal government over what is the right thing to do. These debates can get pretty heated. It's easy to see why, when a state can suffer economically or in some other way, waiting for the U.S. Congress to make laws that are greatly needed, especially in that state's mind, is difficult. Often, states move on and make their own laws. Sometimes, this leads to lawsuits, or overturned laws, or even a trip all the way to the Supreme Court for a "final" decision. But that's ok...a lot of people fought for us to have those very rights. It just means America's "checks and balances" system is working.

The most important thing you can learn in school is to do your own research, read, read, read, think critically, come to your own conclusions—and, most importantly, be willing to have a mind open enough to change when new information dictates that.

...Maryland abolishes slavery...Nevada joins union as free state...Abraham Lincoln wins reelection as president...Sherman begins "March to the Sea" through

Coordinating Committee, led by prominent African American lawyers and activists, announce plans to sue companies that profited from slavery... President George W. Bush awards comedian and actor Bill Cosby and baseball player Hank Aaron

The CIVIL WAR Experience

Good Civil War Books for young readers...

Civil War Ghost Stories & Legends
Nancy Roberts

Civil War Heroines
Bellerophon Books

Book of the American Civil War
Brown, Little & Co.

Civil War Trivia
Edward F. Williams III

The Civil War: Strange & Fascinating Facts
Burke Davis

Dogs of War: And Stories of Other Beasts of Battle in the Civil War
Marilyn Seguin

The Red Badge of Courage
Stephen Crane

Escape To Freedom: The Underground Railroad Adventures Of Callie And William
Barbara Brooks Simon

Rousing Songs & True Tales of the Civil War
Wayne Erbsen

Civil War Book of Facts
Frank Burd

Flags of the Confederacy
Ray DiZazzo

Some Civil War Sites You Can Visit...

Antietam National Battlefield, Sharpsburg, MD

Andersonville National Historic Site, Andersonville, GA

Chickamauga and Chattanooga National Military Park, Chattanooga, TN

Fort Sumter National Monument, Charleston, SC

Fredericksburg & Spotsylvania National Military Park, Fredricksburg, VA

Gettysburg National Military Park, Gettysburg, PA

Harpers Ferry National Historical Park, Charles Town, WV

Kennesaw Mountain National Battlefield Park, Kennesaw, GA

Manassas National Battlefield Park, Manassas, VA

Museum of the Confederacy, Richmond, VA

Pea Ridge National Military Park, Garfield, AZ

Richmond National Battlefield Park, Richmond, VA

Shiloh National Military Park, Hardin County, TN

Stones River National Battlefield, Murfreesboro, TN

Appomattox Court House National Historic Park, Appomattox, VA

Vicksburg National Military Park, Vicksburg, MS & Delta, LA

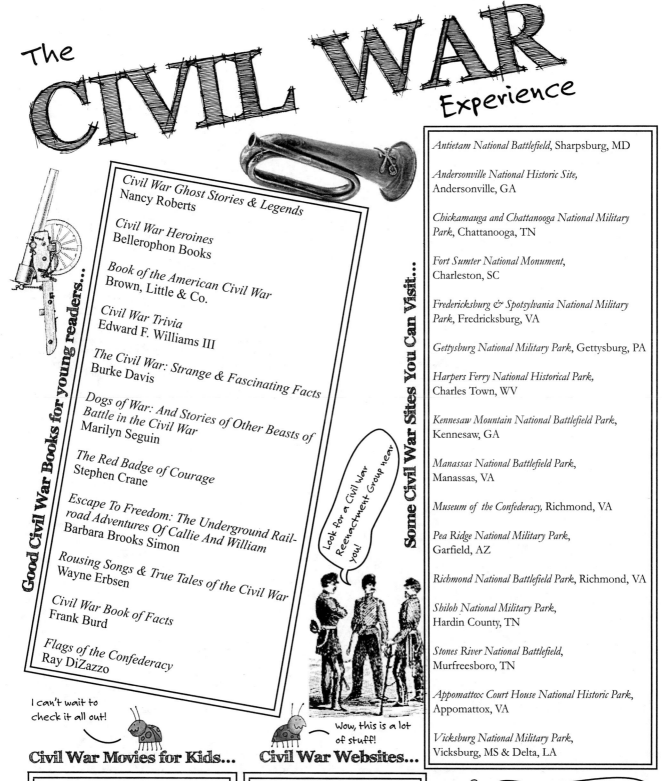

Look for a Civil War Reenactment Group near you!

I can't wait to check it all out!

Wow, this is a lot of stuff!

Civil War Movies for Kids...

The Red Badge Of Courage *(1951)*
The Civil War by Ken Burns *(1990)*

Civil War Websites...

www.studentscivilwar.com
www.civilwar.com
www.americancivilwar.com

Here are just a few things to help you learn more about the Civil War, and maybe even experience it a little!

Georgia...1865...Robert E. Lee appointed general-in-chief of all Confederate armies...Missouri abolishes slavery...Abraham Lincoln rejects Jefferson Davis's

the nation's highest civilian honor—the Presidential Medal of Freedom... 2005... Condoleezza Rice is appointed Secretary of State becoming the first African American woman to serve as Secretary of State...Hurricane Katrina hits southern coast

Please Preserve the Sites!

Civil War battlefields have long stood as silent witnesses to the most devastating war in American history. Today, many face a new enemy—the growth of nearby neighborhoods and businesses that threatens to swallow up precious, historic land.

The Civil War Preservation Trust watches over these sites. Each year, they publish a list of the 10 most endangered Civil War battlefields. Current endangered examples include Cedar Creek and the Wilderness in Virginia, and Gettysburg in Pennsylvania.

What's happening to these battlefields? The Cedar Creek Battlefield faces a limestone mining operation across parts of the historic site. A giant superstore might be built just 1/4 mile from the Wilderness Battlefield. At Gettysburg, a group is seeking approval to build a gambling casino about 1/2 mile from the historic national park.

Why should we preserve Civil War battlefields? These battles changed American history (and possibly world history!) and are part of our national heritage. Preserving these sacred places helps us learn from the men who fought there, appreciate the freedoms they won, and honor their memories.

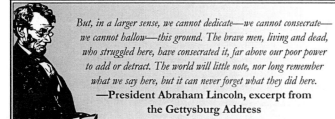

But, in a larger sense, we cannot dedicate—we cannot consecrate—we cannot hallow—this ground. The brave men, living and dead, who struggled here, have consecrated it, far above our poor power to add or detract. The world will little note, nor long remember what we say here, but it can never forget what they did here.
—**President Abraham Lincoln, excerpt from the Gettysburg Address**

If you want to help preserve Civil War parks, visit the Civil War Preservation Trust's website: www.civilwar.org.

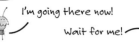

I'm going there now!

Wait for me!

peace proposals…13th Amendment to Constitution abolishes slavery…Confederates forced into full retreat…Confederate general Robert E. Lee surrenders to

of the United States…Ceremonial groundbreaking of the African Burial Ground in Manhattan takes place—the site will serve as memorial to 17th-18th century African slaves…Forbes magazine ranks Condoleezza Rice as the most powerful

Civil War GLOSSARY

abolitionist: *(AB OH LISH UH NIST)* person who believed slavery was wrong and worked to end it

ammunition: *(AM U NEH SHUN)* weapons used during the war such as bullets, gunpowder, shot, and shells

antebellum: *(AN TUH BELL UM)* time period before the Civil War began

army: large group of armed and trained soldiers

battle: major fight between two opposing armies

battlefield: place where battle is fought

blockade: use of military forces to close ports

border states: states that had slavery, but did not secede from the Union

breastworks: temporary fort made of dirt and wood

bummer: soldiers who stole food from civilians

campaign: *(CAM PAIN)* series of military operations

cash crop: crop like tobacco or cotton that was sold for a great deal of money

casualty: *(CA SHUL TEE)* person killed, wounded, captured, or missing in action after a battle

cavalry: *(CAV ALL REE)* soldiers who rode horses

charge: to rush towards the enemy

civil war: war between opposing groups of citizens in the same country

Civil War [1861-1865]: war in the United States fought between the North and the South

colors: flag or banner of a military unit

Good words to know!

Compromise of 1850: series of compromises passed by Congress in an attempt to end the conflict over slavery and keep the Union together

confederacy: *(CON FED DER AH SEE)* a government that favors less federal government and more states' rights

Confederate States of America: *(CON FED DER UHT)* nation of Southern states created when they seceded from the Union

Confederates: Southern soldiers

Copperheads: people in the North who did not support the war

cotton gin: machine that made harvesting cotton easier; invented in 1793 by Eli Whitney

Cotton Kingdom: nickname for the South during the years 1820-1860

Democratic Party: popular political party in the South that believed in states' rights and did not want to end slavery

draft: required men to join the army

Emancipation Proclamation: *(E MAN SI PA SHUN PRO CLUH MAY SHUN)* freed all of the slaves in the Rebel states

enlist: to join the military

federals: Northern soldiers

federation: government of states with a powerful central government

Free-Soilers: people that opposed the spread of slavery

free state: state that did not allow slavery

Fugitive Slave Law: required people in the North to return runaway slaves

Union general Ulysses S. Grant at Appomattox Court House, Virginia…President Lincoln assassination by Southerner John Wilkes Booth…Vice President

woman in the world…2006…The Covenant becomes the first black book to reach number 1 on the New York Time's nonfiction paper back best seller list… 2007…Oprah Winfrey opens the Oprah Winfrey Leadership Academy for Girls in South

Gettysburg Address: speech given by Abraham Lincoln on November 19, 1863

Industrial Revolution [1750-1914]: time period when machines, power tools, and large factories replaced handmade items and small factories

infantry: soldiers trained to fight on foot

inflation: more money is available but the price of goods increases

ku klux klan: secret society organized in the South after the Civil War

manumission: *(MAN U MI SHUN)* when an owner decided to free their slave

Mason-Dixon Line: imaginary line (between Maryland and Pennsylvania) that separated the free states and slave states

militia: *(MUH LEH SHUH)* group of soldiers required to fight only in an emergency

"necessary evil": nickname for slavery by people who did not like slavery but thought it was necessary

North: part of the United States that remained loyal to the federal government—also called the Union

overseer: supervisor who watched the slaves while they worked

parole: *(PAH ROLL)* practice of letting captured soldiers go home—only if they promised not to fight again

"peculiar institution": Southern nickname for slavery

plantation: large farm in the South that grew cash crops and owned slaves

popular sovereignty: *(SOV REN TEE)* belief that the citizens of a state should decide whether that state was a free state or slave state

ration: *(RAY SHUN)* soldier's daily amount of food

rebellion: *(REE BELL YUN)* war where part of the people try to overthrow the government and establish a new one

Rebel yell: *(REH BULL)* cry Confederate soldiers would make before they attacked the Union army

Reconstruction: *(REE CON STRUK SHUN)* time period after the Civil War when Lincoln planned to put the Union back together

"red badge of courage": battle wound

regiment: group of soldiers; during the Civil War a regiment was supposed to contain 1,000 men

Republican party: *(REE PUB LUH KIN)* political party created in 1854 that wanted to put an end to slavery

secession: act of a state formally leaving the United States of America; secession is illegal

siege: *(SEEJ)* when an army surrounds the enemy and forces them to surrender

slave: person owned by another person

slavery: state of bondage where mostly African Americans were forced to work for white masters

slave state: state that did allow slavery

South: part of the country that left the United States to form their own nation; also called the Confederacy or Rebel States

States' rights: belief that states have certain rights that the federal government does not have

surrender: to give up in a battle or a war

sutler: person who followed the army to sell food and supplies to soldiers

tariff: special tax on imported goods

theatre: large area where many battles are fought

Uncle Tom's Cabin: book written by Harriet Beecher Stowe that related the evils of slavery

Underground Railroad: secret route that helped slaves escape from the South

volunteer: person who joins the army because he wants to, not because he has to

Yankee: nickname for a person from the North

All's well that ends well?

Andrew Johnson sworn into office...John Wilkes Booth shot and killed in Bowling Green, Virginia...President Johnson submits plan for Restoration of South

Africa... 2008...Barack Obama wins presidential election becoming first African American president-elect... 2009...Barack Obama is inaugurated as the first African American President ...Michelle Obama is the first African American First Lady...

Reconstruction

Reconstruction: the recovery and rebuilding period following the Civil War

Can you believe the war is finally over? The weight of the world has been lifted from my husband's shoulders. I can see it in his eyes. And we are going to Ford's Theatre to see a play tonight! A night of lighthearted fun—I cannot wait!—**Mary Todd Lincoln**

POP! What was that? Part of the play? Women are shrieking! A man has leaped onto the stage, yelled, and run off. The president slumps in his chair! I see blood! Can it be true?! Did someone just shoot our president?!—**usher**, Ford's Theatre

Stop that man!—**Major Henry Rathbone**

Everyone is sobbing. Our president died early this morning. May God have mercy on this country.—**newspaper reporter**

I accept this office of President of the United States with a heavy heart.—Vice President **Andrew Johnson**

Lincoln Shot!

He was in that barn and wouldn't come out. So we set it on fire! I saw my chance, and took it. I shot him. I shot and killed that John Wilkes Booth.—**Union soldier***

*The manhunt for John Wilkes Booth was the largest in history, involving 10,000 federal troops, detectives and police.

The Legend of *Taps*

In 1862, Union Army Captain Robert Ellicombe looked over the battle scene. He heard the groan of a wounded soldier. Although, he did not know if the soldier was a Union soldier or a Confederate soldier, the captain crawled through the battle amidst gunfire and carried the soldier to the medical tent. When he got back, he found that the soldier was a Confederate, but he was already dead. He recognized the face of the soldier and realized it was his own son. Because the son was a Rebel, he was not allowed to have a full military burial. Only one musician, a bugler, was allowed to play. The father asked the bugler to play a song that was found in the pocket of his son's uniform. The bugler played the song that became known as *Taps*.

This story is legend, not historically accurate

The True Story of *Taps*

General Daniel Butterfield was dissatisfied with the customary firing of three rifles at the end of military burials. He altered a French bugle call into what is now known as *Taps*. The song became very popular, and within months it was sounded by both the Union and Confederate armies.

This story is the true story of *Taps*. Not as fun and romantic as the Legend!

Here are the latest statistics, Sir: 618,000 soldiers dead; probably 100,000 civilians killed too, Sir. That includes the North and South, Sir. And we know that disease killed twice as many as those who died in battle.—**Union soldier ***

*The Civil War death toll is more than the total killed in battle in the American Revolution, War of 1812, Mexican War, Spanish-American War, World War I, World War II, Korean War, Vietnam, and Gulf War— all combined!

When we said our vows years ago, I was just a child. Jefferson was 18 years my elder. My momma almost cried when I said I wanted to marry him. But we've had a happy life together. Full of struggles, I suppose, but happy. I never thought I'd be the First Lady of the Confederacy, not in a million years! But I stand by Jefferson in everything. Right now he's locked up, accused of treason since the great South lost this Civil War. But I'm staying right here outside his jail cell. I'll fight for his release until I feel him back in my arms again, no matter how long it takes.—**Varina Howell Davis***

*Jefferson Davis was released in 1867 thanks to his wife's unrelenting requests for his freedom.

Fields barren. Everything is destroyed! Houses burned. Animals dead or dying—I can count their ribs. What has happened to our beautiful South?— **Confederate soldier**

My lifeless body hangs on the scaffold. Three guilty men wave in the wind beside me. They accused me of conspiring to kill Abraham Lincoln. I did no such thing!—ghost of **Mary Surratt**

If these old walls could talk, they would tell a history so fascinating and terrifying, no student would ever tire of learning about American events. I was built years ago, before any of these men were even born. My walls were erected for protection, but just look at them now. Spirits seem to haunt this sad and forlorn place, and will forever more.—**Fort Monroe**

35

…All Confederate states except Mississippi readmitted to Union…Six Confederate officers form anti-black society, Ku Klux Klan…1866…Congress passes Civil

Susan Rice is the first African American woman to become the United States' U.N. Ambassador… Eric Holder is the first African American Attorney General of the United States… 50-year-old pop icon Michael Jackson dies of cardiac arrest…Venus

We've got to keep these free blacks under control! We'll wear white robes and hoods and terrorize them at night—they'll think we're spirits of Confederate soldiers! That'll keep them in their place.—**Ku Klux Klan member***

* The Ku Klux Klan was a secret society organized by Southerners that used violence and terror to maintain "white supremacy."

Did I ever think I would see this day? No, sir! No more slavery—thanks to the Thirteenth Amendment to the Constitution. What a day, what a day! Free at last! Praise the Lord!—**former slave**

I thought the war was over! But they passed that Military Reconstruction Act and Union troops are still here—occupying the South! It's like pouring salt into a fresh wound. And those Northerners wonder why we're bitter?!—**Southern schoolteacher**

Carpetbaggers! Scalawags! Just look at them taking advantage of our pain to make money for themselves! Why, if one of them comes into my shop, I'll shoo him out so fast his hat will spin right off his head!—**Southern shopkeeper**

Thank ya, suh for these clothes to wear and food for my fam'ly. We have nothin'. Don't know what we'd do without the Freedman's Bureau to help us. It seems like everyone else is ag'in us.—**freed slave***

*The Freedman's Bureau was a federal agency formed to help former slaves get food, clothing, medical care, and fair treatment after the war.

Tenants ain't got no chance. I don't know who gets the money, but it ain't the poor. It gets worse every year—the land gets more wore out, the price for tobacco gets lower, and everything you got to buy gets higher. Like I said, I'm trying to 'be content' like the Bible says and not to worry, but I don't see no hope.—**sharecropper's wife**

We have great hopes for the Fourteenth Amendment! It grants equality to all citizens, but big problems still exist between blacks and whites in the South. Southern states have passed Black Codes—laws to deny former slaves their rights. There is still such violence…will they ever embrace each other?—**Northern Congressman**

So far from engaging in a war to perpetuate slavery, I am rejoiced that slavery is abolished. I believe it will be greatly for the interest of the South. So fully am I satisfied of this that I would have cheerfully lost all that I have lost by the war and have suffered all that I have suffered to have this object obtained.—**Robert E. Lee***

*Robert E. Lee spent the rest of his life as President of Washington and Lee University in Lexington, Virginia

I cannot help but feel sad and depressed…at the downfall of a foe who fought so long and valiantly, and had suffered so much for a cause, though that cause was, I believe, one of the worst for which people ever fought.—**Ulysses S. Grant**

Today, I have been elected to the United States Senate! I'm the first black man elected to the U.S. Senate! I must work to protect the rights of my black brethren. They have a steep hill to climb.— **Hiram Revels**, Mississippi

I'll be the first black man to cast my vote after the Fifteenth Amendment grants blacks the right to vote. My parents were slaves…and here I am! What a privilege! What an honor! I can't wait to vote!—**Thomas Mundy Peterson**

Human nature will not change. In any future great national trial, compared with the men of this, we shall have as weak and as strong, as silly and as wise, as bad and as good. Let us therefore study the incidents of this, as philosophy to learn wisdom from.— Abraham Lincoln

Think maybe the South could win next time?

We lost?!

g'night John Boy

g'night Mama

g'night Tecumseh

g'night Robert E.

g'...

Lights out, boys!

g'night Stonewall

Rights Act…1868…14th Amendment to the Constitution guarantees equal rights…1870…15th Amendment grants blacks right to vote.

and Serena Williams are the first African American world doubles tennis champions…Disney unveils The Princess and the Frog, the studio's first animated film featuring an African American princess.